To: Sandy
It is a pleasure
to know you!
Frank dela Rosa Weaver
March, 2015

Serenades For The Soul
My Life and Yours

Revealing Life Stories Enriching Inspirations

Stories and poems
of a South Texan

Bonus:
Two Spanish Poems
One Sheet Music

Frank De La Rosa Weaver

outskirtspress
DENVER, COLORADO

The opinions expressed in this manuscript are solely the opinions of the author and do not represent the opinions or thoughts of the publisher. The author has represented and warranted full ownership and/or legal right to publish all the materials in this book.

Serenades For The Soul
My Life and Yours
All Rights Reserved.
Copyright © 2015 Frank De La Rosa Weaver
v5.0

Cover Photo © 2015 thinkstockphotos.com. Interior images Dreamstime, LLC All rights reserved - used with permission.

This book may not be reproduced, transmitted, or stored in whole or in part by any means, including graphic, electronic, or mechanical without the express written consent of the publisher except in the case of brief quotations embodied in critical articles and reviews.

Outskirts Press, Inc.
http://www.outskirtspress.com

ISBN: 978-1-4787-4894-6

Library of Congress Control Number: 2014922126

Outskirts Press and the "OP" logo are trademarks belonging to Outskirts Press, Inc.

PRINTED IN THE UNITED STATES OF AMERICA

Dedication

These poems are dedicated to you, the reader, as I humbly embody the life and existence we all share to form the fabric of their creation.

My special thanks to my wife (Oralia), my family and our special friends, who I have thanked personally, for their encouragement and direction without which this work would not have been completed.

About the Author

Frank (De La Rosa) Weaver was born in 1944 to Ramon Cavazos Weaver and Odilia De La Rosa in Santa Maria, Texas. Frank speaks both English and Spanish fluently. Frank's great grandfather, Henry George Weaver, came to Texas from Pennsylvania around 1845 when the U.S. was guarding the border with Mexico. He was a physician. Dr. Henry George Weaver married Maria Alcala of Monterey, Mexico, in 1855. They settled in the area of El Venadito a small village on the Old Military Highway (Texas Highway 281) about 20 miles west of Brownsville, Texas. Frank's father Ramon was the son of Henry G. Weaver II and Margarita Cavazos of an area near El Venadito.

Frank's mother Odilia De La Rosa was born in Santa Maria, Texas, to Lauriano De La Rosa and Rafaela Salinas. They were early immigrants from Mexico around the time when Pancho Villa was raiding the border towns on both sides of the Rio Grande River (1910-1920). Odilia's father, Lauriano, had a family grocery store which he relocated frequently from one side of the Mexican border to the other to avoid Pancho Villa. In this area the last raid was in Mexico; that determined the fate of the family to remain north of the border. The northern fate, however, was not always good; during the great depression Lauriano lost large sums of money he had in the bank. Bank accounts were not government insured at that time.

As a young man, Frank worked in a 'cotton gin' in the Rio Grande Valley of South Texas, in his Radio and TV Electronics repair shop and in various jobs for his parents. Some of these jobs included tending their 'grocery store', running 'film projectors' for his Dad, and tending a 'pool hall' also for his Dad. At Saturday nights' local gatherings he worked as 'disk jockey' at his father's public dances when his father did not have a live band to play in the dance patio, a green colored cement slab surrounded by bougainvilleas as hedges and side benches for the women. This time in Frank's life was from 1952 to 1960. The dance place was called 'Patio Las Bougainvilleas' in Santa Maria, Texas. Most people within 20 miles knew of the dance place and came in large numbers from the larger communities and farms. Many local Mexican-American bands called, 'conjuntos', played there.

In 1963, Frank graduated from La Feria High School, La Feria, Texas, completing electronics correspondence courses while still in high school. He earned a Bachelor of Science Degree in Electrical Engineering from Texas A & I University in Kingsville, Texas, in 1968. During his studies at A&I, Frank was chosen to be a cooperative education student with NASA Johnson Space Center in Houston, Texas. After graduation he was hired by NASA where he worked as an Aerospace Engineer.

Frank married Oralia Palacios from Concepcion, Texas, in 1968. She was born to Raul Leal Palacios and Manuela Morris Garcia. Frank and Oralia have two sons, a daughter and seven grandchildren.

Frank is a former Texas Registered Professional Engineer. In 2001, he retired after 36 years with NASA. In 2004, he and his wife moved to Concepcion, Texas, where they own and operate a family ranch. He enjoys private flying and restoring antique radios. He became a member of the Kleberg County Airport Advisory Commission in 2010. VTCI (Valley Telephone Cooperative Incorporated) headquartered in Raymondville, Texas, appointed Frank to the Board in 2012. Subsequently, he was elected by the VTCI membership to remain a Board of Director. He has been an active member of the Immaculate Conception Catholic Church in Concepcion, Texas, since 2004. He believes in the importance of giving back to his home community – South Texas.

Frank's varied interests, experiences and background give him a unique perspective on life and people that he now shares with heart felt scenarios played out in his inspiring poems.

Introduction

This book is about the life and struggles of the author and the life encounters he observed in society. Those events are expressed in stories called 'settings'. The accompanying poems cry out those life struggles and life encounters in rhyme which pull on the heart and seek the acceptance of God.

In a way, this book teaches by example by revealing how the author (and others in some cases) dealt with life's doubts, fears and successes. Written snapshots of the life stories are accented by the strength of a poem. The author's life revealed is that of a hopeful American that trusted his hold on society only to his abilities and knowledge gained in his young years, in school and in the University. To him it was like a swim upstream at times, but he took the challenge.

These life stories are what he leaves to his family, relatives and friends as they were not always in the struggle to see what he saw, to feel what he felt. He prints it because it echoes what other people have felt and experienced and describes the events so as to help the readers understand their own existence. Hopefully the reader will find comfort and direction in their personal lives by seeing that they are not the only ones who have had those feelings and situations. His story is your story in many ways.

The author is an instrument rated private pilot. He

brings his experiences of being a pilot, with its attendant methodologies, to the book. He writes of flight in one of his poems and reveals the background for his writing. He brings the discipline of being a pilot to his writing by being as honest as possible in describing the events and background for his writing.

The writings invariably speak of personal human love and of God's love and security. They give God all the praise and thankfulness for having made it in "the play", so to speak, for having been given the opportunity to live and relate to others on this earth for His glory and purpose.

Preface

There are moments in our lives that leave us with joy, others leave us with thoughts of who we are and our own purpose. And then there are moments when we reflect on tragedies in life and try to bring meaning to those events by turning to God.

The poems include life scenarios many may have in common. Some life scenarios are my own and some are general observations. It is my hope that the reader will be enriched by the life events depicted and thus add value to their own lives.

Each of these poems is preceded by a brief writing of the life event it portrays and by what I saw as the source of its inspiration.

Contents

Life 2

Days of Joy 6

My Love 10

Will You Take Me Back Again 14

Wonderful Day 18

Houston Streets 22

Nature Leads 26

That Beautiful Voice 30

Get Well Wish 34

Mother's Day 38

Judgment 42

God's Mercy 46

Peoples of the World 50

On Valentine's Day 54

Oralia 58

Wonder Begets Wonder 62

A Thanksgiving Day Apart 66

The Other Life 70

The Wonder of Flight 74

Dreams 80

Don't Take it Wrong 84

Me and My Sun 88

That Stirring Hope 92

Like Perfect Friends 98

Jewels Among The Cacti 102

Prayer for Defense and Justice After WTC Incident 9/11/2001 108

Un Amor Sin Hablar 116

Mi Corazón 122

Life

Life

Life, Setting

This poem was written well into my working career. Three kids and a wife made it a home in this large Southeast Texas town, Houston, Texas.

I was 18 years into my life. The life I talk about is one that includes more than just the job that carried us financially but the whole life set of 'family and job'.

I believe we all come to moments in our lives when we reflect on who we are and where we are going. I often wondered what we were doing there away from relatives and school friends to raise a family and meet our expectations of life. By 'expectations of life', I mean actualizing our education and training for a better life. That was my inspiration.

Yes, it is in this setting that this poem was created. I think we all reflect on this theme, if only for a few seconds, as we go through life's struggles. This is how I expressed it in this seemingly ageless modern American 'way of life'. It was 1988.

Life

Abrupt and pure the tree protrudes,
Above the life of purple hue,
To rest among the lowly ebb, of water.

Beyond the limbs are bountiful herbs,
Distilled in luminous water flow,
Too deep to gather, too soft to touch.

We go unnoticed from to and fro,
Astride a wind directed flow;
It leads to there but where is life?

To me the world at times is still;
We move but get no where at all;
The things we treasure far we keep,
And think of daily and dream in sleep.

Days of Joy

Days of Joy

Days of Joy, Setting

There are times in which we find ourselves in very spiritually quiet settings or moments in life where we would like to stay forever and enjoy the peace and tranquility. These moments could be found when we first wake up in the morning or when we have periods during the day to relax. But soon some thought rises or someone calls us to something that needs attention outside of ourselves. Those events snatch us away to the 'real world' once again.

My inspiration for this poem was the great life condition at that time. As much as I would relish the idea of explaining to all what those moments mean and why we have them, I must keep myself out of the realm of things I know little about. The essence of our spiritual and physical existence and the interworking of that I must defer to the trained individual and ultimately to God himself.

I find that my memory of most of these experiences is of short duration and fleeting and must be captured quickly if it is to be revisited. Such was the moment described in this short poem for that fleeting moment. It was the fall of 1967. I was 23 years old.

Days of Joy

The days of Joy and Laughter,
Are here to come again;
The rain outside like tears of Joy,
Sing out the coming chain,
Of thoughts so sweet to linger,
Beside a fire place,
To be among the happiest,
In this human race.

++++++

The days of Joy and Laughter,
Now have come and some are gone;
But not the Maker, not our God,
Whose light continues on.

To bring more joy and laughter,
As He once so plainly said,
My yoke is easy, My yoke is light,
My joy....My joy forever after.

Frank De La Rosa Weaver

My Love

My Love

My Love, Setting

It was a rainy night. It had been a long day at the office. Coming home, I called my wife before leaving work and heard the voice of one wanting to see me. She was tending to three kids with homework and had just finished routing them to and from school extra curricular activities.

It seemed as though all was done. The kids in bed and sound asleep I poured a glass of wine for two and sat with her to watch the news on TV. It was about 10:20 pm and the weather forecast was about to start.

I knew she needed reassurance and I felt I was still in love with her. I enjoyed her company more than even at the beginning of our married life.

I told her how I felt about her. After the night was over I sat down and wrote this poem to record the moment before its memory fled.

My Love

Chain in me a memory;
Cry a tear of rhapsody;
Lunge to me your love dear;
Breathe a whisper in my ear.

String your lines across my body;
Tie your bow against my soul;
Take of me all that you savor,
My passion, my lover, my world.

Never think that I would leave you;
Let your love relentless show;
Press your thoughts and mine together,
And feel my love within you grow.

Frank De La Rosa Weaver

Will You Take Me Back Again

Will You Take Me Back Again

Will You Take Me Back Again, Setting

The plight of too large a number of young people that find themselves cast into this world from dysfunctional families inspired me to write this poem.

These young people, some children, struggle often times without being aware of what they are missing from supporting parents. They do what they can 'as is' in school, in society and in their spiritual life.

I sense that this poverty of parental guidance and of not learning the ways of God leaves them to grow up spiritually and socially deprived.

Unfortunately, they often do not acquire a good concept of right and wrong. They frustrate the laws of conduct of our society and ultimately the laws of conduct of God.

In this poem a young person, who having been left without the support of parents at a young age, finally clamors for God's acceptance and security.

Unfortunately, that person finds itself to be immersed in, what is believed to be, a cruel world.

Will You Take Me Back Again

Alone while very young,
Took the world on nonetheless;

Never lost sight of your hand;
Those days were not so grand;

To err is human, yes they say;
But yet it's no excuse;

The guides you left me, left me too;
I kept my sight on you, my friend;
But still,
I'm asking Lord, will you take me back again.

Frank De La Rosa Weaver

Wonderful Day

Wonderful Day

Wonderful Day, Setting

Love was on my mind as I wrote this poem. As an inspiration source, love came through as I was appreciating the days in which I lived at that time. It was 1994.

The flowers are symbols as even smiles are. The flower expresses the inner working of the plant and the smiles the inner self of the person.

June is, of course, a good month for green grass and flowers. The flowers that spring suggested are now accepted by summer, welcomed and nourished.

I reflect on the love that brought on the spring, that produced that flower and the love that projects in a smile.

However, it is not love itself that is being celebrated but its results, i.e., smiles, flowers and everything in this world that has a beginning and an end. And yet, even though love is not being celebrated, love is the source essential ingredient and is being shared with all of humanity.

Wonderful Day

Flowers are silly like smiles;
June is coming near;
Days like these are what we cheer.

The days can come and we don't ponder;
We miss the wonder of the Love of God;
We celebrate his handy work;
Then, we see his wonder.

I wish to share what knows no dates,
Knows no end and no beginning,
It cannot have a festive day.

What God has made is what I share;
Love on this wonderful day.

Frank De La Rosa Weaver

Houston Streets

Houston Streets

Houston Streets, Setting

As I mentioned earlier, my wife and I had thrust ourselves into the life of Houston, Texas.

As in many large cities in the U.S., many different people from other parts of the world made their home there too. Having come from a small town in South Texas, I considered before arriving in Houston that my social challenge was going to be difficult. However, I figured that the social fabric would still be composed of the same type of people I had been used to, just more of them. I was wrong.

In the NASA space program, where I made my work career, there were people of different National origins and parts of the U.S., another element to contend with and to understand.

Houston Streets

The moon, the hill, the obstacle glow,
You look around and wonder,
to know,

If those around are really your own,
Or sprayed out before you,
From a distant land,

To confuse the wandering heart,
To separate the deliberate plan.

You hear the talk , you see,
The plays;
Daily it seems people are dazed.

It's change! It's conflict!
It's the Houston streets ways.

Frank De La Rosa Weaver

Nature Leads

Nature Leads

Nature Leads, Setting

It was the fall of 1993 and as I sat at the nature camp grounds of Lake Livingston State Park in East Texas, I reflected on the direction of my life and wished to be lead by the wisdom found in the ways of nature.

In the intervening months since we had been to this park, life in the big city had been, as is usually the case, filled with efforts of mankind to build lives, pay bills and do the other expectations of life. All of this commotion, though necessary to survive, is usually 'hectic and noisy'. It is like finding one's way through a determined crowd to get to the other side.

Not complaining, but rather reflecting, since people in general generate the needs that we the working class meet and solve. Meeting those needs allow us to earn a comfortable living. Nonetheless, I was longing for a more perfect existence. From such desire came the inspiration for this poem.

There is little controversy that God's animals can and do teach us about a life that depends on Him. Indeed the birds neither labor nor exert yet God provides for them. To me, people are to do the same. People to a greater extent do well if they implement their skills and work to solve other's problems with love. In this manner mankind will rarely go without.

Nature Leads

Noise from man abounds,
From thunder of his will,
Too silent to understand,
Too loud to be heard.

Your river runs but you,
Must see,
That what you hear is the will
Of man,
Off tune with nature and its plan.

Instead do as the birds;
Follow in tune and do their way;
The lasting will,
The light from God.

Frank De La Rosa Weaver

That Beautiful Voice

That Beautiful Voice

That Beautiful Voice, Setting

It was the spring of 2013 and local restaurants were competing for the best food and the best ambience.

We began frequenting a new Mexican restaurant that had been opened by a family from Jalisco, Mexico, to taste the unique flavors and enjoy the hospitality of the owner/family. It seemed as if we were visiting them personally when they greeted us at the restaurant. That friendliness made us feel 'at home'.

It was here that we would come to hear local singers who had been doing well in their singing careers.

I wrote this poem one evening as the singing session was ending while sitting at one of those restaurant tables.

That Beautiful Voice

The sound of that beautiful
Voice,
Lifts the spirit of many;
The smile brings joy to all;

The crowd is surprised as they hear,
That beautiful sound so near;

The songs of others are prized,
With the melodious enchanting Voice;

The evenings go sweeping by,
As they come to listen by choice;

Enriched in their souls, they sigh,
Cause they heard,
The sound of that beautiful Voice.

Frank De La Rosa Weaver

Get Well Wish

Get Well Wish

Get Well Wish, Setting

This is a light hearted poem I was inspired to write about a singer who had come down with a bout of the flu.

We had enjoyed many of the performances. The singer moved the crowd so much so that the absence, even though temporary, was felt by all.

It was not long thereafter that we were able to hear the great songs once more.

Get Well Wish

I hope you feel better;
I wish you were fine;
The angels are waiting,
In care all the time;

To see you uplifted,
And graciously sing,
Songs from the heart,
That give us a fling.

The stage makes you fly;
Your songs make us cry;
Your heart pours out feelings,
The crowd finds appealing.

You must get well soon;
Come give us a whirl;
Yes soon you'll be flying,
And yes.....we'll be crying.

Frank De La Rosa Weaver

Mother's Day

Mother's Day

Mother's Day, Setting

There is no love greater among mankind, in my opinion, than the love of a mother for her sons and daughters.

Certainly rare, except among women, is that love that is resident in every mother. There are many possible ways to have described that love in different words in this poem but they would all have arrived at the same end.

Like a light, mothers shine upon their siblings and the comfort lasts their lifetime. Lucky are those of us who are able to say that their mom is still alive today. But to support the rest of us it must suffice to hold that she loved us like a light shone from above.

In reality, this poem was written by a husband about his wife instead, the mother of their children. The children are now grown with lives and families of their own. Fortunate is that mother to have these few words from their father to pass on to her children.

I wouldn't know just how long to make this poem and be able to fully describe a mother's love. As you can see, even these extra words are no closer to doing her justice.

Mother's Day

Hearts are rare,
That care like you,
That smile and think,
Like rays of blue.

Like radiant light,
Above the morning,
Creating bright,
Our hearts belonging.

You share your life;
You give it too;
So young and old,
Can see you're true.

You make the cloudy day,
Fill up with sun you do;
The day becomes your smile;
Your smile becomes our day!

Frank De La Rosa Weaver

Judgment

Judgment

Judgment, Setting

As a Christian I was taught that each one of us will have to answer to our creator in some way upon death.

To appreciate this poem one must be of the belief that there is a creator. That that creator will someday have us account for our actions on this earth. That at the end of this life we are to be given a new life elsewhere for the purpose of God. And to be prepared to do God's will in a new existence, we must have demonstrated our commitment to God's ways.

One day at the age of 40, I was sitting on the back porch watching a beautiful sunrise. I had a desire to express in words what I felt to be a truth.

Judgment

Like the river you run forever,
Like the dew falls from the vine,
As when darkness yields to dawn,
You befall like rays of sunlight,
To the depths of untold minds.

Like the trees near the river,
You hug us we can tell;
You want us to be true,
And to deliver well.

To be truthful of our life,
To kneel before Your mercy,
To come clean before You Lord,
To tell You every word.

To incline our heads anew,
To the Love against we sinned,
If not planned nor secret plotted,
He will see the heart in me and you.

Frank De La Rosa Weaver

God's Mercy

God's Mercy

God's Mercy, Setting

It was the fall of 2013. I had accumulated several poems which I shared with the pastor of our church. He read some of them, paused and went on to the next ones.

After he read the poem on 'judgment' and possibly several of the others as well, he told me that since I already had a poem on 'judgment' that I should write one on God's mercy also. I took that on as an interesting challenge and wrote the poem attached.

Contrasting, I suppose that God's judgment can be a very frightening experience. I was either not thinking of the consequences of which I wrote when I wrote 'judgment' or I didn't believe that I would end up getting a 'bad score' from God. God seems to offer mercy so we can get to heaven. Given the state of man and given God's ways, I consider that 'judgment' without mercy would be very destructive. I understand that to break one of His commandants is to break them all.

Truly, I am grateful God did not leave heaven up to us alone. I have come to realize that humans fall short of reaching heaven on their own. We are material and spiritual beings in a world made of matter. What seemingly keeps us 'surviving' is the material. But to go to heaven, I have read, means dying to the things of the world, opposing conditions at best.

Thank God for His Mercy.

God's Mercy

Mercy is the want of my Soul,
A virtue reserved at creation;
For our Father's love to mold,
His great plan for salvation.

Accept His mercy we must,
We are weakened, unable to speak;
Yet in Him we are able to trust.

God, you have given us time to believe;
Your parables meant to clear us the air;
For us to forgive and receive,
Your Mercy and loving care.

Please complete your promise to me;
I seek your ways and repent to be,
One striving to keep from offending thee.

And thus knowing your love,
Would receive Devine Mercy,
And be rescued above.

Frank De La Rosa Weaver

Peoples of the World

Peoples Of The World

Peoples of the World, Setting

Many young people in our modern society 'transplant' themselves and their family to large cities to find good paying jobs.

When my wife and I moved to Houston, Texas, we knew no one around us when we started. We made friends; but it was not the same since we had grown up in a tightly knit community in South Texas.

In the environment of Houston, Texas, and with the job of working in the space program, I felt driven to work side by side with people not only from the United States but from other countries in the world. The task was compelling and exciting and I felt fortunate to be part of the struggle to excel in the space program. We needed to beat the Soviets to the moon. In effect, the United States of America had placed itself in a difficult position. We were to beat any other nation that might dare to take preeminence in space. This was done in the interest of our national security.

So the inspiration for this poem came from the excitement of taking part in a task for a greater purpose. I was aware of the natural tendency to want to make life count; that itself generated pressures in the journey.

Peoples of the World

Nature's own melody, chains of cells,
Compose the poise of ether,
And sound, as if to push outward, and far;
It makes itself real, abounds and stands,
In windows of time, one at a time.

The outer sphere is like a foe;
We are here together on a ship,
And on a journey as we go.

Inescapable as in a wall,
And the waters separate, as if to pause,
The force that binds us one and all.

Frank De La Rosa Weaver

On Valentine's Day

On Valentine's Day

On Valentine's Day, Setting

It was 1964 when I first met the girl that I later married. Some time lapsed between that first meeting and the second 'tag up' in the fall of 1967.

We were both attending college in Kingsville, Texas. It was called Texas A&I University then. Later, it took on the name, Texas A&M University at Kingsville.

In 1964, I thought she didn't seem very interested in me. I later found out that it was her shy personality that held her back from expressing a real liking for me. In fact, she kept track of me through a cousin of hers. I would 'disappear' on her, she said, on several of those semesters between 1964 and 1967. She did not know I was a cooperative education student alternating semesters of work and study with NASA, Johnson Space Center in Houston, Texas.

Nevertheless, I asked her out and she accepted to go to the fall homecoming game of the 'Javelinas' in 1967. We were now seniors in college. The courting began then. I met her parents in the next few months. Her mother liked me a lot but her father really did not want his daughter to marry too soon. He had envisioned that she was going to help with the family finances once she graduated. Months went by.

We were both waiting to finish school to get married. It was Valentine's Day 1968. I gave her this poem as an expression of my love and to give her hope for our future.

On Valentine's Day

On this day that lovers everywhere,
Share in thoughts of cupid's deeds,

I bring to you this message,
With red hearts lined with flower seeds.

Indeed, the hearts are but a symbol,
Of the real heart that feels;

For what could ever symbolize,
Your love that gives me thrills.

Save the seeds for when you're sad,
Your tears may fall on them instead,

And make them bloom in many ways,
To bring you joy and beauty to your waiting days.

Frank De La Rosa Weaver

Oralia

Oralia

Oralia, Setting

This is a poem about my wife and soul mate. She is keener on natural affection feelings such as those expressed in words and deeds rather than on rings and pretty jewelry. Of course she admires a beautiful ring, necklace or bracelet but those things are not as valuable to her.

We were now 45 years into our marriage. The kids had kids of their own. We had moved away from the big city lights to the tranquility and pace of a South Texas town. It was a small unincorporated town but had a post office, a small store and a Catholic Church.

In the midst of church activities, volunteering and ranch life, I was inspired to write a poem about my best friend and wife, Oralia. I must admit, writing those words also gave me a renewed sense of confirmation of what was there all along.

Even though our kids are now grown with families of their own, they are lifted and feel secure in the words of this poem.

Oralia

The waves may roar;
The ship may sway;
But not my love,
Through all the day.

Our love is sturdy;
It's a rock on earth;
It's wide and deep,
As the ocean's berth.

Though rains may come,
Though lightning strike,
The rock is steady,
And holds its ground;
As my heart to yours,
My mind and yours,
Are one and bound.

Our children are gems,
Our gift from God,
To guide and nourish,
To see their children,
Run, smile, and flourish.

Frank De La Rosa Weaver

Wonder Begets Wonder

Wonder Begets Wonder

Wonder Begets Wonder, Setting

This poem is about life and a point in my life when I was trying to synchronize the physical existence with the spiritual being inside.

In a simplistic way I have, at times, made the analogy of a car to our bodies when thinking of the body and the spirit. The car has a driver inside like our bodies have a spirit inside. Certainly the car and driver must become one for that purpose for which they are combined. Similarly, the body and its spirit combination must act as one to arrive at a pleasurable end.

I was 30 years old when I wrote this poem. Even though I was following my heart and my vision at the same time during this point in my life, I found that this was being done for the most part by faith in God. However, the things I occupied myself with were material with a beginning and an end.

Suddenly, my course found me defining the sole essential source of my will and my drive. By using the example of the material around us and following the guide of the power of God and the force of the universe, one can achieve a moderate level of satisfying destiny. I reflected on the thought that this material universe is, after all, God's creation, a creation from which we can receive vigor and thus be inspired to author some level of wonder in our own existence.

Wonder Begets Wonder

The will to do, the will to make,
Like instinct, like reflex,
We cannot see,
Where we wish to go or be.

Yet, as if we knew, but,
Unaware of the bigger plan;
Yet a plan, would someday end,
If it once begin.

No! It's more than that, it's Love, in motion;
As the sun loves us by shinning,
As the earth feeds us to live,
Both sustain us as an example,
That we too must live to give.

So imitate the Wind! The Stars! The Sun!
The plentiful and power,
Of a revolving planet!

We must be following God's Guide,
So that wonder begets wonder,
And we're in symphony in that stride.

Frank De La Rosa Weaver

A Thanksgiving Day Apart

A Thanksgiving Day Apart

A Thanksgiving Day Apart, Setting

As many families are at times separated due to jobs and other matters, we came upon our Thanksgiving Day in 2013 without all children being at our home, the parent's home.

Such a day gave me the motivation to write this poem and send it to our children.

This poem was intended to give them and us a sense of togetherness and love. We made several attempts at being together for that Thanksgiving celebration. Unlike most of our other Thanksgiving Day gatherings, this one did not happen.

A Thanksgiving Day Apart

In this good Thanksgiving Day,
Even though we're apart,
We all know from the start,
We're together at heart.

Our hearts are together,
Like the breeze on a tree,
Hugging it gently and true;
We write this message today,
Especially for you.

We felt we needed to write,
These words before they fled;
Or stay lying in bed,
Thinking of you instead.

In spite of the distance and miles,
We remember and picture your smiles;
We know you are well,
And continue to tell,
That our love is what keeps us so dear;
Though apart we all sense we are near.

Frank De La Rosa Weaver

The Other Life

The Other Life

The Other Life, Setting

At the age of 44, I was reflecting on the life we live on this earth from the perspective of being victorious in that effort.

My inspiration came from the belief that we are known by God before birth on this earth. I believe that we were made with certain abilities to help us survive.

In this earth's existence, therefore, we as a species overcome and subdue the earth and its creatures and are victorious in that effort. However, I believe we are not to be victorious for our own glory, for if we were, we would not be wise and sincere.

The Other Life

No one goes unnoticed, no one dies;
From heavenly count we surely flow;
The everlasting code is here;
The young and old will long endear.

To be apt, to be ready,
I go to ends and see no better;
Walk by the river and do not gather,
Life where is there life?

Cope with fear, man has invented,
To make you stronger in its might;
You cannot conquer and be wise;
You cannot win and be sincere.

The sun is gone, the wind blows hard;
It has no mercy, we are tested well;
The day will change, we will survive;
Again we must endure, again.

The Wonder of Flight

The Wonder of Flight

The Wonder of Flight, Setting

Once, when I was about 6 years old, I got a toy jet fighter for my birthday. It had wheels that when made to roll would create long sparks out of the rear opening; it was a single engine jet.

That left an impression on me at that early age and may have been the reason I later obtained a private pilot license for single engine propeller airplanes.

I had a dream one night in which I was flying right seat with another pilot as in a night flight from Oklahoma City to Houston, Texas. In my dream, I clearly saw written across the instrument panel of that plane the words: "Where Does One Draw Some Such Men". Written below and to the right of that phrase was the name of the author of those words; the name, both first and last, started with the letter "A" but I could not make out the rest of the letters. The words I saw on the plane's instrument panel are what motivated me to write this poem. I hope I am being fair to that phrase and that I am giving it the respect it deserves.

The Wonder of Flight

One dreary night, half past ten,
Whisking the still of the air,
The clouds were dark and dense;
The need for skill was there.

Smug in the cockpit we flew;
Harsh elements screaming outside;
And just as the story would read,
A splendid flight indeed.

Switching from controller to another,
From Ok City to Houston we pushed;
The warm city lights below were grand;
Wished we never would land.

With two pilots up front,
Auto pilot set to the goal,
We reminisced the grandeur of flight,
The fullness of life becoming the soul.

We wish to pass some of this on,
For others to experience this too,
To share from these gifts,
To raise our spirits to you.

Continued

To see the wonder of flight,
To sense the beauty and might,
To dwell closer to God,
And sense his inviting light.

Nearing Houston Center,
We hear the tower of Hobby;
Awakened now to that fact,
To land, to land we must;
But, yes, we'll be back.

Dreams

Dreams

Dreams, Setting

I must confess this poem was not planned. Like an unexpected child birth to a married couple, it just came. Sometimes those can be the best, the ones in God's plan and timing.

The inspiration for this poem came from my own struggle with dreams. I tend to analyze events in my life. Dreams seem like real events at the time they happen. Sometimes I remain aware of a dream as the day progresses to see if there is a meaning to it.

I regard a dream about myself as bad if it presents a scenario of fear. I would not follow a dream like that. On the other hand, a dream with inspiration and promise in my life is one I would like to see lived out.

Dreams

Dreams that come to you,
Once they make it known,
Space your mind that day,
And want to have their way.

Always check them out,
For some are good and some are not;
Take of them what helps you out,
Leave the rest to fade instead.

Hitch your favorite to a star,
Watch it zoom and take you far;
Hold on tight and keep your trust,
Keep, keep that hold you must.

When you get there give a smile;
Put a thankful heart and show,
That on you it was poured,
That blessing few will know.

Frank De La Rosa Weaver

Don't Take it Wrong

Don't Take It Wrong

Don't Take It Wrong, Setting

I was inspired to write this poem after having seen the experience of many young people who have many ups and downs in their love relationships.

Possibly because of feelings of inadequacy for deserving the other's love or for a variety of other reasons, one or the other is misunderstood for the real feeling they have for the other.

Don't Take It Wrong

Don't take it wrong,
When you hear that I don't love you;
Don't take it wrong,
When they say that I don't care.

The day will come,
Our love will come to stay;
Don't take it wrong,
I love you all the way.

Inside my heart,
The whole of me is aching;
It feels for you,
My patience slowly breaking.

Don't get it wrong,
Because you see me free;
My dreams are yours,
And some day you will see.

Your tears will dry;
My lips and yours will touch;
My love is yours;
I love you, oh so much.

Frank De La Rosa Weaver

Me and My Sun

Me and My Sun

Me and My Sun, Setting

Our community (Concepcion, Texas) was having a fiesta in May 2014 to raise funds to build a church hall.

The area is predominantly cattle country with horses kept for working cattle and for pleasure. The area is what is called 'brush country' around South Texas. It abounds with mesquite and prickly pear.

At that time the church was producing a fiesta 'program' to distribute to people as they would come to participate. The church parish was looking for a poem to go in that 'program' handout. I volunteered to provide a poem for the program.

This poem was inspired by the setting of the area and by the end goal of the church and its proposed new hall building, i.e., winning souls for the Lord.

Me and My Sun

The sun rises alone,
As I too ride alone.

The hoofs of my horse,
Gracefully take the course,
To his destiny.

As I too go to mine,
I seek Your face among mesquite;
I find You there among the cacti;
The thorns You endured for me,
What You suffered to set me free.

Of sin's bondage You paid the price;
For me to live instead of die,
For me to rise not alone,
But with You by my side.

Frank De La Rosa Weaver

That Stirring Hope

That Stirring Hope

That Stirring Hope, Setting

I have no clear idea what inspired this poem. I can take a stab at it this way. My wife believed that since I had the hope of publishing these poems that I was putting down my own recipe. That could be true but she too had a lot of church work to do as president of a church organization tasked with raising money for a church hall.

So maybe both of us had a 'stirring hope'. But people in general often have hopes of achieving something for themselves or for others. I like to think that it was because of <u>their</u> hopes that I was inspired to give some words of motivation.

That Stirring Hope

When there's a hope that stirs you,
When there's a work upon you,
Take your strength and go;
Show your friends you know.

We seem small, but take the step;
Steps are small, and that's OK;
Go beyond the mark;
Stumble not your start.

Seek a vision and remember,
It takes only little work;
Think your plan as fun,
God will follow, just go run.

Leave your doubts aside;
Plan your passion with your drive;
Let your vision be your fuel,
The strength within your stride.

Take your life as being none;
Wash your mind of trouble;
Clean your hands of all unclean;
Your life and you will double.

Continued

Thankful always be,
You made it in the play;
You let Him direct, you see;
You let Him show, the way.

Like Perfect Friends

Like Perfect Friends

Like Perfect Friends, Setting

We had moved back to my wife's (Oralia's) home town in South Texas to come back to our roots. We had lived and worked in the Houston area for 36 years. The decision to move was not made lightly. It was difficult to decide to move back and leave our sons and a daughter who were spread out from Dallas to Houston. But move we did after we visited her hometown one day and learned of 45 acres of land that had come up for sale. It had deer and many other wild animals.

The property belonged to a distant cousin of my wife. They needed to sell so they could afford to buy a tract of land that would give them road access to another property they owned nearby. We built a house on these 45 acres and enjoy the private setting of ranch life with another tract of land my wife had inherited.

This poem was written about a couple who lived in this South Texas town we moved to after retirement. They were very dear to us. They owned a ranch nearby and had some cattle.

We started our new life in South Texas and learned many things from this couple. We learned about raising cattle and white tail deer hunting.

This friendship continues to this day. I wish to honor that friendship with this poem. They were my inspiration.

Like Perfect Friends

You welcomed us like perfect friends;
You helped us learn the way;
You kept a place aside,
For us to fit and do,
For us to here abide.

With ranching things to learn,
To make a life we searched,
You helped us find the ropes;
You helped us win our hopes.

The hunting lessons came in time,
As they were needed they were mine;
The finer things of shooting you told me,
To round my know-how don't you see.

Friends like these are very kind,
Who take you without cause,
Who share a life they've come to love,
A life to see us find.

The years since then been ten,
The number since we met;
The dinners had together,
The hopes we cared,
Enriched the lives we shared.

Frank De La Rosa Weaver

Jewels Among The Cacti

Jewels Among The Cacti

Jewels Among the Cacti, Setting

Before I mention the couple that is the subject of this poem, I wish to say that the couple from the poem "Like Perfect Friends" had to spend many weeks living in Austin, Texas, to make routine visits to medical facilities. We had many enjoyable years of knowing and helping each other with ranch chores. Even now they remain our very dear friends.

Well, about the time that we were seeing less of the couple who spent a lot of time in Austin, we met some new friends which I fondly refer to in this poem as the "Jewels Among The Cacti". We wish we had met them earlier since we have many things in common and we really enjoy their company and family.

Feeling very fortunate to have made their acquaintance, I was inspired to write this poem and let them know about it.

Jewels Among The Cacti

Like stars above the sky,
Like comets streaming by,
They shine and keep us bright;
They leave a comfort sigh.

Where have you all been before?
We never saw you through the years;
No glimpse of you, no word at all.

Guess you were hiding in the brush,
Beneath mesquite with cactus near;
God waiting for the proper time,
To let us see your light,
To let you be so dear.

You seem to act with so much care,
A love of friends that's very rare;
We hope we measure up to that;
So very lucky that we met.

The weeks and months go by and all;
We learn of you the more and more;
The more we do, the more it seems,
We fit and lift each other's dreams.

Continued

To God we owe these charming friends,
To angels carrying his commands;
We now request His blessings done,
No stone to trip our steps;
Only light and good blessings be,
The paths we take to thee.

Prayer for Defense and Justice After WTC Incident 9/11/2001

Prayer for Defense and Justice After WTC Incident, 9/11/2001

Prayer for defense and Justice after WTC Incident 9/11/2001, Setting

This prose was written by a father whose daughter had a very close call by this incident. Only 10 minutes of time separated her from disaster as she had just taken the subway leaving the World Trade Center in New York City. Only a father can know the feeling I had as the event was taking place. My daughter finally called to say she was alright but she could not get back home by plane since all air travel had been halted.

Filled with frustration and emptiness of strength, I began expressing my understanding of the 'fabric' of the people that caused this incident and how that played in the context of my deep Catholic Christian religious belief.

The perpetrators, though dead themselves, had a significant following and ideology that I attempted to address. In doing so, I turned to God and prayed that He remember who we were as a nation and how this other ideology needed to come to his attention immediately.

Imploring to God for help, I proceeded with this writing with the trust that this United States of America, having been formed by a God fearing people and having had the hand of God shape it with people from around the globe, would rise with the support of our Godly faith to put a stop to this type of violence.

At the same time, I felt that the rationale the enemy used to do this in the first place needed to be understood to begin a dialog of truth.

Prayer for Defense and Justice After WTC Incident, 9/11/2001

GOD, you asked us to be slow to anger because,
all people are Your children.
That we are not fighting flesh and blood but
"powers and principalities" unseen.
But GOD, You have also warned those by whom
evil befalls on another.

We know we are all sinners in this world,
no one excluded.
You sent Christ and offered him as the way
to reconcile all of us to You.
You did this for all peoples of the world,
regardless of their creed then and now.

It costs nothing to accept Your gift of grace,
only our belief and obedience.
That we are to love one another and share
this world amongst ourselves for our good
And Your glory.

Lord, our response to the embassy bombings
we have kept to the law of justice.
With the "USS Cole", we have done Your will
by turning the other cheek.

Continued

However, they have bruised it too, because,
they don't fear You.
They use Your commands upon us as shields,
and with them they form daggers to afflict us.

Lord, while You shaped our character by Your will,
You also made us powerful to overcome those,
who would use that against us.

Yes, there are greedy among us here and
across the world.
But the afflicters do not see the 'log'
in their own eyes while they pretend to remove
the 'speck' in our own.

We have been a caring Nation around the world,
and respect the sovereignty of countries
that govern themselves by the choice of their people,
rather than ruthless dictators.
Even the latter we don't use as an excuse to plunder
a nation.

It is time now… to ask you for Your help,
to allow us to defend and protect
this country You have shaped with many
peoples from around the world.

Continued

So help us GOD, for we intend now to do this,
to obtain justice for our nation,
and for the nations of the world
who are and can be affected by this
manner of violence.

And not only to obtain justice, but to plant
a mighty Deterrence,
so that this Nation and others who do Your will
can endure for Your glory and for the life,
of righteous people of all complexions.

Un Amor Sin Hablar

Un Amor Sin Hablar

Un Amor Sin Hablar, Setting

This poem came through my pen in less then five minutes. It was not like the ones that developed after several days or weeks of encountering life events and people.

Looking for a title to this book and having made little progress, I switched gears, so to speak. After an hour of that search, a search that included help from my wife, I began outpouring this poem like no other before in my experience. (I had learned Spanish in my early years.)

It was only after writing it that I had my first impression of what I thought inspired it. I concluded that two young people, a girl and a boy in their mid-twenties, were looking at each other across a reception room of some wedding they had been invited to.

Like love at first sight, the young man looked at the girl until their eyes were locked. At this point she smiled as if she had known him already before. Eyes still locked he began to know her and she looked down, as if holding back, and came back up to look at him again and both smiled once more.

As if she was calling him, telling him she was already fond of him, he answered her silent call without talking at all. He recites the event in this poem by introducing it in the first stanza and expressing his unspoken words to her in the last four stanzas.

A different twist:

A friend of ours had a different meaning for this poem. As soon as she heard it for the first time she said, "It's the Holy Spirit." She told us that the Holy Spirit is the one talking, saying <u>all</u> of the words. That the Holy Spirit was communicating to us without spoken words of its own.

Un Amor Sin Hablar

Un amor existió;
Sin hablar me llamó;
Me dijo que me queria;
Sin hablar le contesté.

Ven a mi sin palabras;
Envuelveme con amor;
Sube las mas alturas,
Y no me enseñes tu dolor.

Sigue tu corazón;
Siempre escucha tu visión;
Dame tu cariño lento,
Como un amor sin hablar.

Canta ya tus esperansas;
Estrecha tus brazos así a mi;
Abre tu cariño sólamente,
Como un amor sin hablar.

No me dejes mi cariño;
No te vayas ya de mi;
Por que ya te conocí,
Como un amor sin hablar.

Mi Corazón

Mi Corazón

Mi Corazón, Setting

It's a reality in this world that people sometimes live lives for a time that bring them great mental/emotional and physical pain.

My inspiration came from the suffering and tormenting life of a person. However, in the end, that person brought on a celebration of pain overcome and personal growth of wisdom acquired.

In overcoming this pain the person gives thanks to the Lord. The person is not bitter, and even reflects on the personal growth of going through that suffering . Then that person thanks not only God, but thanks all humanity and offers a heart to comfort and guide others through their life experience.

Mi Corazón

Mi vida fue un tormento;
Mi vida fue un dolor;
Que hora doy sin precio,
Y todo con amor.

Después de aver sufrido,
Después me levanté;
Di gracias al Señor,
Que aquel dolor se fue.

Con mucho nuevo amor,
A pesar el dia sin cumplir,
[Ya] Aprendí a levantar,
Y a mi prójimo ayudar.

Con mucho Corazón,
Y mucha reflexión,
A lo que me formó,
Para dar mi Corazón.

CPSIA information can be obtained at www.ICGtesting.com
Printed in the USA
BVOW04*1330220215

388680BV00006B/30/P